FEB 2 2 2005

Music Math

Exploring Different Interpretations of Fractions

Kathleen Collins

PowerMath™

The Rosen Publishing Group's
PowerKids Press™
New York

Published in 2004 by The Rosen Publishing Group, Inc.
29 East 21st Street, New York, NY 10010

Book Design: Michael Tsanis

Photo Credits: p. 5 © Bill Varie/Corbis; pp. 6 (stopwatch), 12, 13, 28, 29 © Eyewire; p. 6 (sheet music)
© C Squared Studios/PhotoDisc; p. 17 © Ted Streshinsky/Corbis; p. 18 © Mark Adams/Taxi; p. 21 ©
David Zickl/SuperStock; p. 30 © Alvis Upitis/The Image Bank.

Library of Congress Cataloging-in-Publication Data

Collins, Kathleen.
  Music math : exploring different interpretations of fractions /
Kathleen Collins.
       p. cm. — (Powermath)
Includes index.
Summary: Explains math fractions by means of musical notation.
  ISBN 0-8239-8984-4 (library binding)
  ISBN 0-8239-8877-5 (pbk.)
  ISBN 0-8239-7386-7 (6-pack)
  1. Fractions—Juvenile literature. 2. Musical notation—Juvenile
literature. [1. Fractions. 2. Musical notation.] I. Title. II. Series.
  QA117.C64 2004
  513.2'6—dc21
                                        2003002242

Manufactured in the United States of America

Contents

Composing Music

The people who write music are called **composers**. Composers use a special language called **musical notation** to write music. The notes used in musical notation are like the letters and numbers we use when we write. Musicians must be able to read musical notation in order to know what sounds to play, what the **rhythm**—or beat—should sound like, and what the **tempo**—or pace—of the song should be.

In order for musicians to know how to play the music, they have to be able to read the notes and count the beats. Understanding math is useful to both the composer and the person who plays the music. Just as numbers tell us how to count in math, notes tell us how to count in music.

Musical notes are like whole numbers and fractions. Just as whole numbers and fractions can be added together to form new numbers, whole notes and note fractions can be added together to create a new song. Read on to learn more about music math.

6

A musical **composition** is measured in a way that is very much like the way we measure time. We divide time into hours, minutes, and seconds. These **units** represent a part, or fraction, of larger units. For example, an hour is $\frac{1}{24}$ of a day because there are 24 hours in a day. A minute is $\frac{1}{60}$ of an hour because there are 60 minutes in an hour.

Music is measured in a similar way. In music, "time" means the way a composition is divided into smaller units. A song is divided into lines, **measures**, and notes. Just as hours, minutes, and seconds are the units of measurement we use when we talk about time, lines, measures, and notes are the units of measurement we use when we talk about music.

Some clocks, like a stopwatch, break time down into tenths and hundredths of a second. The smaller a unit is, the less time it takes for that unit to pass. Musical notes can also be broken down into smaller units that last for shorter periods of time.

Note Values

Each note in a song is like a number or a fraction. The "largest" note is the whole note. You might think of a whole note as the number 1. A whole note looks like a hollow circle.

Whole notes can be broken down into smaller notes. A half note looks like a whole note with a handle. A half note lasts $\frac{1}{2}$ the time of a whole note. A quarter note looks like a solid circle with a handle. A quarter note lasts $\frac{1}{4}$ the time of a whole note and $\frac{1}{2}$ the time of a half note. This means that the time it takes to play the whole note is equal to the time that it takes to play 4 quarter notes.

An eighth note looks like a quarter note with a flag at the end of the handle. An eighth note lasts $\frac{1}{8}$ the time of a whole note. A sixteenth note looks like a quarter note with 2 flags on it. A sixteenth note lasts $\frac{1}{16}$ the time of a whole note.

whole note = 𝅝

half note = 𝅗𝅥

quarter note = ♩

eighth note = ♪

sixteenth note = 𝅘𝅥𝅯

thirty-second note = 𝅘𝅥𝅰

sixty-fourth note = 𝅘𝅥𝅱

There are even thirty-second notes and sixty-fourth notes, though they are not used very often. A thirty-second note is $\frac{1}{32}$ the length of a whole note. A sixty-fourth note is $\frac{1}{64}$ the length of a whole note. This means that in the time it takes to play a whole note, a musician plays 32 thirty-second notes or 64 sixty-fourth notes!

whole note = **2 x** 𝅗𝅥

whole note = **4 x** ♩

whole note = **8 x** ♪

whole note = **16 x** 𝅘𝅥𝅯

whole note = **32 x** 𝅘𝅥𝅰

whole note = **64 x** 𝅘𝅥𝅱

9

whole rest =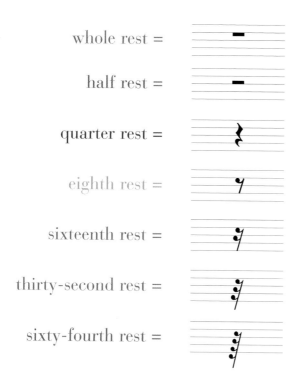

half rest =

quarter rest =

eighth rest =

sixteenth rest =

thirty-second rest =

sixty-fourth rest =

Think about one of your favorite songs. Imagine what that song would sound like without rests between the notes. Or, imagine rests that are of different lengths from the rests that are normally there. This will help you see how changing rests can change the song itself.

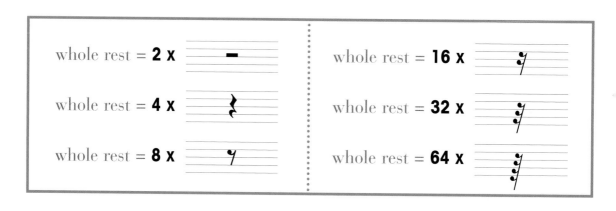

whole rest = **2 x**

whole rest = **4 x**

whole rest = **8 x**

whole rest = **16 x**

whole rest = **32 x**

whole rest = **64 x**

For each type of note—whole, half, quarter, eighth, and so on—there is also a matching **rest**. A rest in a musical composition is a period of time when no note is played. Rests last for the same number of beats as the notes they replace. Even though musicians don't actually play music during rests, rests are still an important part of the composition.

Rests can be broken up just like notes are. A whole rest lasts the same amount of time as a whole note. A whole rest looks like a black bar attached to the bottom of a line. A half rest lasts $\frac{1}{2}$ as long as a whole rest and looks like a black bar attached to the top of a line.

A quarter rest lasts $\frac{1}{4}$ as long as a whole rest. This means that a whole rest, 2 half rests, and 4 quarter rests are all equal. There are also eighth rests, sixteenth rests, thirty-second rests, and sixty-fourth rests.

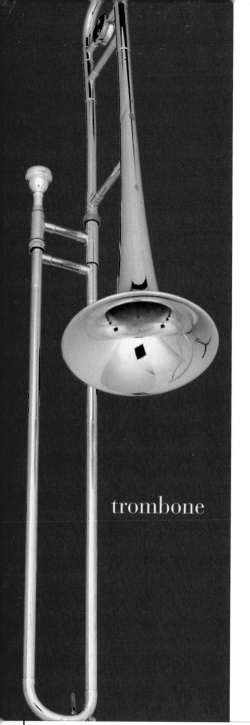

trombone

Sometimes you will see notes and rests in a musical composition that look like whole, half, and quarter notes and rests with a dot next to them. A dot beside any note or rest increases its value by half the original value. For example, imagine that a whole note is 4 beats long in a composition you are playing. If it has a dot next to it, you add half of the original value. Half of 4 beats is 2 beats. So in this case, a dotted whole note is 6 beats long.

If a half note is 2 beats long, a dot adds 1 beat to it. So a half note with a dot next to it is 3 beats long. If a quarter note is 1 beat long, a dotted quarter note is $1\frac{1}{2}$ beats long.

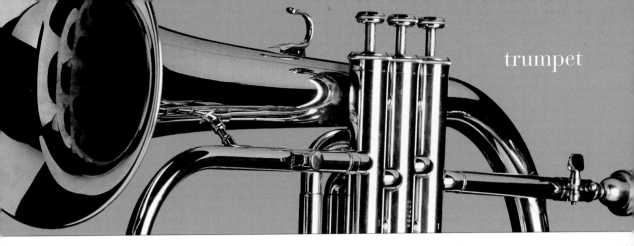

A dotted eighth note is $\frac{1}{16}$ longer than a regular eighth note. This is because $\frac{1}{8}$ equals $\frac{2}{16}$, and half of $\frac{1}{8}$ is $\frac{1}{16}$. So, a dotted eighth note is equal to 3 sixteenth notes.

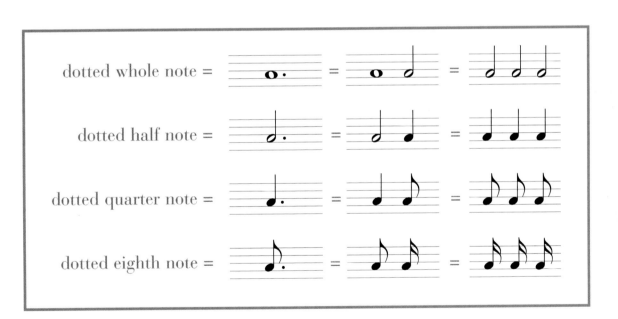

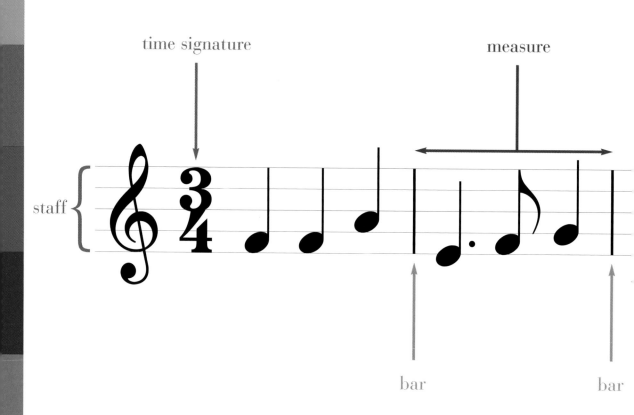

Musicians know which tones to play based on where a note is positioned on the lines of the staff. A note can be on a line or between 2 lines. Some notes can reach above the top line of the staff. Some notes can reach below the bottom line of the staff.

Time Signatures

Music is written on a musical **staff**. The staff is the 5 lines and the 4 spaces between them on which music is written. The lines of the staff are divided into measures that are separated by bars. At the beginning of most songs, you will see something that looks like a fraction written on the staff, except that there is not a line between the top number and the bottom number. This is called the **time signature**.

The time signature is a quick way for the composer to explain the kind of rhythm the song has and how long the different notes last. The time signature tells musicians how the measures of the composition are divided throughout the song. Without a time signature at the beginning of a composition, a musician playing the song would have no way of telling how many beats were supposed to be in each measure. The song could be played dozens of different ways—all of which would sound different—but only one of them would be the way the composer meant for it to be played.

15

The top number in the time signature shows how many beats there are in each measure. For example, a time signature with a 4 on top means there are 4 beats in each measure. A time signature with a 3 on top means there are 3 beats in each measure.

The bottom number of a time signature shows which type of note will receive 1 beat. For example, a time signature with a 4 on the bottom means that a quarter note is equal to 1 beat. A time signature with a 2 on the bottom means that a half note is equal to 1 beat.

So a $\frac{4}{4}$ time signature means there will be 4 beats in each measure and each beat will be represented by a quarter note. A $\frac{5}{2}$ time signature means that there will be 5 beats in each measure and each beat will be represented by a half note.

Rock and pop music usually use a $\frac{4}{4}$ time signature. Marches are often written in $\frac{2}{2}$ or $\frac{2}{4}$ time. The $\frac{3}{4}$ time signature is sometimes called "waltz time" because it is the time signature used most often in waltzes. However, plenty of songs that are not waltzes have a $\frac{3}{4}$ signature. Country music is often in $\frac{3}{4}$ time.

17

To figure out what type of note gets a beat, just replace the top number of the time signature with a 1. For instance, a $\frac{6}{8}$ time signature would mean that an eighth note ($\frac{1}{8}$) gets a beat. It also means that there are going to be 6 beats in each measure. A $\frac{3}{2}$ time signature means that a half note ($\frac{1}{2}$) gets a beat and there will be 3 beats in each measure.

Another way to look at the $\frac{3}{2}$ time signature is to say that there will be 3 half notes in each measure. A $\frac{3}{4}$ time signature means 3 quarter notes per measure. A $\frac{5}{2}$ time signature means 5 half notes per measure. A $\frac{6}{8}$ time signature means 6 eighth notes per measure.

The most common time signature is $\frac{4}{4}$, which is sometimes called "common time" because it is used so often. If you don't see a time signature at the beginning of a song, you might see the letter "C" instead. The "C" stands for "common time."

Musical Fractions

Time signatures look like fractions, and this may cause some confusion at first. It may seem strange that a time signature of $\frac{3}{2}$ means that there are 3 half notes in 1 measure. You might think that since 2 halves make 1 whole, a whole measure couldn't have more than 2 half notes. Just remember that while 2 half notes equal 1 whole note, a measure can have whatever number of notes the composer decides they want it to have. Think of it like a recipe. A whole cup of sugar always equals 2 half cups—no more, no less. However, a recipe may call for $1\frac{1}{2}$ cups—or $\frac{3}{2}$ cups—of sugar.

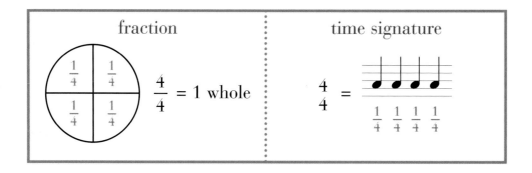

The fraction $\frac{4}{4}$ represents 4 equal parts out of 4 total parts, or 1 whole. The time signature $\frac{4}{4}$ is different. "Four-four time"—or "common time"—means that each measure has 4 quarter notes and each quarter note equals 1 beat.

"My Country 'Tis of Thee"

words by Samuel F. Smith, 1831

My country 'tis of thee, sweet land of liberty, of thee I sing. Land where my

fathers died, land of the Pilgrim's pride, from every mountain side, let freedom ring.

treble or G clef =   bass or F clef =

"My Country 'Tis of Thee"

Let's study this composition and see how everything works together. The first thing we should look at is the time signature: $\frac{3}{4}$. This means that this composition has 3 beats per measure and each quarter note gets 1 beat. Notice that the first measure has 3 quarter notes, or 3 beats. The third, fifth, seventh, and ninth measures also have 3 quarter notes.

Notice that the time signature $\frac{3}{4}$ is different from a math fraction. In math, $\frac{3}{4}$ means 3 equal parts out of a total of 4 equal parts of a whole. In this case, $\frac{3}{4}$ tells us that a single measure equals 3 quarter notes. If you played this song, you would count to yourself: "1, 2, 3, 1, 2, 3, 1, 2, 3," and so on.

The figure at the beginning of each line of music is called a clef. A clef tells musicians what each note should sound like. The most common clefs are the treble or G clef, and the bass or F clef.

The only note in the sixth and fourteenth measures is a dotted half note. Remember that a dot beside any note increases its value by half of the original value. Since a half note in this composition has 2 beats, that means that a dotted half note has 3 beats: $2 + 1 = 3$.

Measures 2, 4, 8, 10, and 12 all have the same arrangement of notes: a dotted quarter note, an eighth note, and a quarter note. We know that these measures have a total of 3 beats each because the time signature is $\frac{3}{4}$. Let's see how the notes add up to 3 beats. A dotted quarter note equals $1\frac{1}{2}$ beats. An eighth note is $\frac{1}{2}$ of a beat. A quarter note is 1 beat. Now add them together: $1\frac{1}{2} + \frac{1}{2} + 1 = 3$. A measure with these notes has a total of 3 beats. What other kinds of notes and note combinations do you see in this composition?

sixth measure

dotted half note

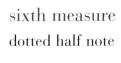

2 beats + 1 beat = 3 beats

second measure

dotted quarter note, eighth note,
quarter note

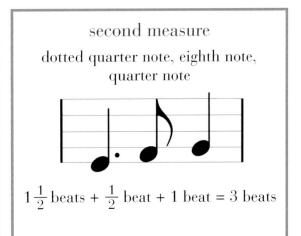

$1\frac{1}{2}$ beats + $\frac{1}{2}$ beat + 1 beat = 3 beats

In measures 11 and 13 there are notes connected by curved lines. These curved lines are called "slurs." The slur tells the musician to play these notes so that they flow smoothly together.

eleventh measure

quarter note, 4 eighth notes

$1 + \frac{1}{2} + \frac{1}{2} + \frac{1}{2} + \frac{1}{2} = 3$ beats

thirteenth measure

2 eighth notes, quarter note,
dotted eighth note, sixteenth note

$\frac{1}{2} + \frac{1}{2} + 1 + \frac{3}{4} + \frac{1}{4} = 3$ beats

"Auld Lang Syne"
traditional Scottish song, words recorded by Robert Burns, 1788

Should auld acquaintance be forgot and never brought to mind? Should auld acquaintance

be forgot. And days o' auld lang syne. For auld lang syne, my dear, for

auld lang syne, we'll drink a cup o' kindness yet for auld lang syne.

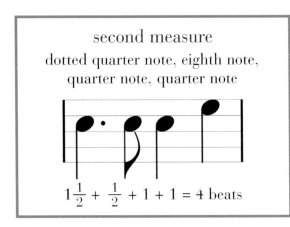

second measure
dotted quarter note, eighth note,
quarter note, quarter note

$1\frac{1}{2} + \frac{1}{2} + 1 + 1 = 4$ beats

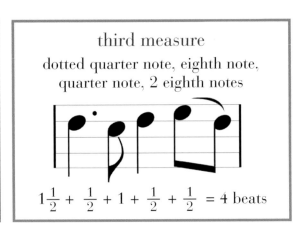

third measure
dotted quarter note, eighth note,
quarter note, 2 eighth notes

$1\frac{1}{2} + \frac{1}{2} + 1 + \frac{1}{2} + \frac{1}{2} = 4$ beats

"Auld Lang Syne"

The time signature on this composition is $\frac{4}{4}$, which is also called "common time." That means that there are 4 beats in every measure and each quarter note gets 1 beat. The easiest measures to count are the fifth, ninth, and thirteenth measures, which have a dotted half note (3 beats) and a quarter note (1 beat). If you played this song, you would count to yourself: "1, 2, 3, 4, 1, 2, 3, 4," and so on.

Let's take a closer look at other measures in this song so we can see how the notes add up to 4 beats per measure. Measures 2, 4, 6, 8, 10, 11, 12, 14, and 16 all have the same arrangement of notes: a dotted quarter note, an eighth note, and 2 quarter notes. Altogether, these notes add up to 4 beats.

Measures 3, 7, and 15 all have the same arrangement of notes: a dotted quarter note, an eighth note, a quarter note, and 2 eighth notes. Do those notes add up to 4 beats? Yes!

"Auld Lang Syne" is a traditional Scottish song that was first recorded by a Scottish poet named Robert Burns in 1788. It has become a favorite song to sing at midnight on New Year's Day. The phrase "auld lang syne" means "times long gone."

violin

Notice that the first and last measures are not a full 4 beats long. The first measure is only 1 beat long and works as a lead-in to the song. The last measure is 3 beats long. Together, however, they equal 4 beats. This is so the song can be played repeatedly as new verses are sung. When the final measure ends, the musician can begin the song again without losing the beat.

Notice that the half note and quarter note in the last measure are connected with a curved line, just like slurred notes. When 2 notes of the same **pitch** are connected with a curved line, it is called a tie. Tied notes are played as 1 long note. How long do the tied notes in the final measure last? The answer is 3 beats.

Compare the compositions on pages 26 and 22. How are they different? How are they the same? For what types of occasions might people play these songs?

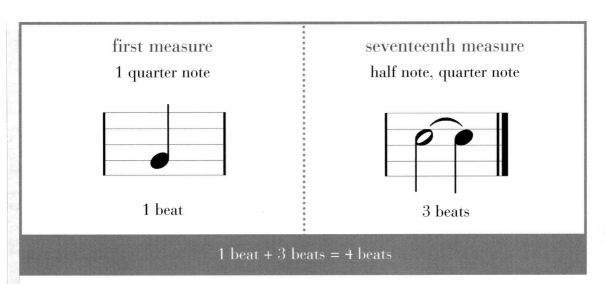

first measure

1 quarter note

1 beat

seventeenth measure

half note, quarter note

3 beats

1 beat + 3 beats = 4 beats

acoustic guitar

Music Math

As we have learned, fractions in music and fractions in math are different in some ways. The time signature, which looks like a fraction, is not something that you can divide, like a real fraction. In math, the fraction $\frac{3}{4}$ can also be expressed as .75 or as 75%. That is not true for a musical fraction. However, music and math fractions also have some similarities. In math and in music, fractions are added up to reach a whole number. For example, in math, the fractions $\frac{1}{2}$ + $\frac{1}{2}$ equal 1. In music, 2 half notes equal 1 whole note. Do you see any other similarities between math and music?

Glossary

composer (kuhm-POH-zuhr) A person who writes music.

composition (kahm-puh-ZIH-shuhn) A piece of music.

measure (MEH-zuhr) The space between 2 bars on a musical staff.

musical notation (MYOO-suh-kuhl noh-TAY-shun) The system of
marks used to write down music.

pitch (PICH) How high or low a sound is.

rest (REHST) A period of silence in a piece of music.

rhythm (RIH-thum) The pattern of sounds in a piece of music.
The time signature and the tempo help to create the pattern
of sounds.

staff (STAF) The 5 lines and 4 spaces on which music is written.

tempo (TEHM-poh) The speed at which a piece of music is played.

time signature (TIME SIG-nuh-chur) Numbers written at the
beginning of a musical composition to indicate the number of
beats in each measure and the type of note that gets 1 beat.

unit (YOO-nuht) A standard amount by which things are measured.

Index